Verses of Flame

Selected Works of Ryan M. Duke
aka Gabriel Samadhi

Table of Contents

Chapter 4: The Prose..157

Chapter 1

Mystic and Practical Inspirations

Dreams That Inspire

Shaking off sleepy memories
still conversing in the dream world
a classroom for those in slumber.

The unconscious mind
burning off worries and preoccupations.
Oh, the meaning we seek
from what sticks upon awakening.

Do you ever ask yourself,
"Whose dream are we?"

When that day comes
when each of us are startled into the awareness
of a new life,
what mental constructs will you take with you?

The dowry of the mind and soul
it is ever written with the actions we take
and the perceptions we cling to.

Do not laden your karma
with unnecessary suffering.
Do not spit in the face of God
by causing harm.

All things are remembered,
and all things will be paid in full
when we awake from this final dream.

Thoughts on Modern Living

I have stripped away all programed standards
of reason and judgement
that are based within a societal sense of normalcy.

Take unto yourself the wisdom
of an ageless truth
that is solidified
in the core of the human condition.

Finding myself alone in disagreement
with every status quo.

When what is in error becomes standard
the fact that it is an error becomes lost
to the knowledge of the collective.

People regularly mire their souls in bondage
for various faiths, principles, or ideologies
and think nothing of it
when they cast aside the sacred for what is acceptable
in their small bubble of awareness.

Damnation's snare
has invisible threads.

The thirst for knowledge must have no agenda
and find no place within
what the ego seeks to justify.

Don't let your morality become lost in the sauce
of some shit someone else taught you
to think and believe.

Each soul answers to itself
according to its own weight.

All Things in Rise or Decline

All things in rise or decline
Coming into being and passing away

The physical is impermanent
The spiritual will transfigure
But the mind will make its mark

The death mask charade
Panics the nimble leap frog logic

An idiot's delight
Buttery manna for the ego
There is pleasure and there is passion,
be careful how you mingle them

Clinging to the fear of what we cannot define
we poison our own well
What variation do you wish to destroy

Vet your beliefs well
For they will betray you

Where there is fear seek understanding
Open what is closed
Love

Spring Renewal

All has thawed for spring
All is alive and flourishing in their way
The weather is inviting, even the showers refresh

Nature exudes its own ancient tranquility that precedes humanity's
artificial hives of bustling congregation

We know we must return
To remind ourselves of the true wonder of our world
when we find it undisturbed

All is Ripe for Awakening
(Samma-Sambodhi)

I've got the look
that scares away demons

Can you look yourself in the mirror and systematically dismantle all
you thought was true, everything you believed to be real? Can you
deconstruct the patterns of rationale and logic to see where their true
motivations are rooted?

Can you look the devil in the eye and say, "You're completely full
of shit, be-gone from our midst, you insolent fool?"

As Buddha said in the Dhammapada, Chapter 11: Old Age and
Death, "Vainly I sought the builder of my house through countless
lives. I could not find him . . . how hard it is to tread life after life.
But now I see you oh builder! And never again shall you build my
house. I have snapped the rafters, split the ridgepole, and beaten out
desire. And now my mind is free. There are no fish in the lake. The
long-legged cranes stand in the water."

The Alchemy of a Moment can Sustain a Universe

A mind seeking the great liberation
should not place itself inside the veil of attachments
that come along with the classifications of form
if one hopes to ever manifest ones eternal incarnate energy of the
soul
which in its purest essence needs no form
and when fully actualized and illuminated
with the precision of a great thunderstorm
the soul can be projected into any living being
hence, shape-shifting

If you fear no entity living or dead,
angel or demon
then you elude all arenas of evil
for if you attain this you take the water from the roots

If your will is stronger than and more vast than your physical reality
then it is possible to make what you will into reality
in the concepts of the ancient magicians
summoning the four corners of the universe
the upper and most parallel self knows
what it will always know, and all throughout time must comprehend
what the conscious self may call intuition
Decipher the natural chemistry of that and you may feel
all the security of Heaven

When you meditate on these things you may be finding yourself
on the thresholds of what people call psychic

Society has enslaved its collective mind
in a fabricated world that has detached its energy
from the elements of existence

Establish your identity from within and then externalize
to find peace from within
Shine with a spiritual radiance for all the world to see

Cleanse Your Karma

I have tasted death on more than one occasion
and I have witnessed death more times than I care to recollect

That final release
a mystifying horror
To those who know the oxygenated states of the human brain
death does not change so much as it transforms.
For energy cannot cease to exist and there is the 21 grams factor
but the weight of the soul is not something that can be measured by
quantitative human means.
Like a garland of endless flowers,
fashion as many good deeds from your life as you possibly can.

Nothing but compassion will save us
no one but you can do it.
We all have to start our path with the same step

We cannot stand apart
we must live together
The truth is as plain as the nose on your face
and we all know it
And deep down we all know, we all know it
so stop trying to ice skate uphill
Consider the complexity of the statement
Do not judge by any standards. Allow an objective understanding of
reality to form within the concept of your personal reality.
Then allow that point of view to temper your gut reaction.
Cause the least amount of suffering that you possibly can, this is the
path to a state of grace and wisdom

You have to reach past all the physical conditions to attain the state
of pure Heaven.
Few will have the will and bravery to delve so deeply, it is not a
state of mind, it is not a state of consciousness,
it is a state of being within all levels of consciousness.
That is to say it is the state in which all conscious beings intersect.
Time catches up with all of us

What time did you reserve for understanding?
Deliver yourself from the tide of Samsara,* plunge threw the waves
of fear and desire
For you will not be doing so blindly
But with the spearhead of God's love.

*the indefinitely repeated cycles of birth, misery, and death caused
by karma. (Merriam-Webster.com)

To Take Flight

Delving into the bottom
in quicksilver glimpses of non-reality
inner reality
subject to hypnotic immersion

Stepping back from the trance that insights daydreams
a separate reality merges with the day unaware

In perfect stillness the soul rises
within the presence of the earth entirely

The Page has Turned

Endless
expectations
englobing
the mind

Laughing
mantras
relinquishing
the heart

I am going home
to make a new start

The Green Fairy

Where will the moment that delivers the onslaught
of crowning virtue begin its un-limitable course?

For virtue when truly present in the heart
becomes the most monumental cause in one's
scope of understanding

It will be the moment when you feel the most securely and
openly revealed
without cause nor expectation

The revelations of Heaven present themselves
among your own thoughtless action.
Established in infancy, but
dis-acknowledged in the infamy of the ego.

When can each of us exist in the presence of everything we affect
without states of doubt, or consequences?
When will each of us take account of the degradation of selfhood?

If you can perceive your reality beyond your own
individual internal awareness
all the external energies become a part of how you
conduct yourself,
transcending inherent karma, into states of blessings

Revealing the presence of forever within but a moment,
time has no basis in death.

Be true to all who encounter your better nature
until the only thing that exists within you
is your inherent nature,
the sweet breath of Samadhi.
Then you will see the presence of
God in the totality of now

Esoteric Musings

Why does the Western
world consider ponderous
meditation a waste of time?

The time we have
to live and breathe

idle time
time for action

My massive daydreams simmer
on the bake light asphalt of reality

One translucent
perception of what
is happening
must not be clung to
pass along the death and birth
of each breath

The heart beats eternal
though the earth recoils
and one day we will never
wake from this dream

Realization determines your level of consciousness
both in life and death
How many societies have come into being, flourished and declined,
then transpired
into evolution nothing more than an artifact?

How long has this crazy trip we call humanity
been rewriting its fears for each new generation
still firmly repressed by the last?

With our baser impulses
and fears rearing their heads
into ideology and outlooks

even humanity will one day
see itself out of the cycle of rebirth

Maybe when we reach a day of common omnipresent understanding
and compassion for all things
there will be no place for this thought experiment any longer
The progress that has been made is considerable
but the sun has not yet set
and the shadows are dwindling into the light

A Chattering Tooth Ramble

moments of dis-acknowledgment from the
present never reveal their most
intimate roots

to merely be inspired with distractions
with my myriad of dear ones of a soulful acquaintance
I will always know dependable
stalemates to rebuke the internal fire

though it is in my nature to displace
the pulp of my heart in the decadence
of a glance, of fleeing moments
I must bid them blessings
that my presence cannot place

such brisk imagined moments sprawl
through the shell of my inherent tendencies
until they themselves manifest
me

so what shall be conceived of this plane
the disjointed sentiments of Angels propagate
in the fleeing fathomless daydreams of mortals

saints and psychotics alike know they are only
being imagined notion to notion
within but a single moment of heaven

Realizations Conquering Despair

Semi-lucid daydreams
take my subconscious and run away with it please.
The embers of my memories have been feeding the fire
for far too long.

When I withdrew from the world I unknowingly was rehashing
the karma and experiences from previous lives.

I have come to the resolution that my inner world is going to reign
over the outer.
What we are taught to be important, in the grand scheme of things,
often doesn't matter a damn. It frequently amounts to a crock of shit
a lot of times, and it almost always involves the ego.

The secret truths of this world are the saddest most devastatingly
painful things one can ever come to realize, but the final peace of
eternal paradise is unattainable unless they are fully actualized
within the soul and mind. It is the prerequisite I feel.

I write these words for myself, but also in the hopes that some may
take benefit from reading them in the future.

That's true of all I write.

Buddha said:
"Thousands of candles can be lit from a single candle, and the life of
that candle will not be shortened. Happiness never decreases by
being shared."

A Word Experiment

condescend
consent
sensualize
epitomize
totally
exemplify
why
your enerrr-
gy
burning
sooooo
ooo
trUE
in
its
own
hypothesized
space
to
  o
b   b
and
    e   e
w   v
     a
amidst
thought

We All Want to Get Into Heaven

wrangling the
rancourous
thoughts
that begin and end
with the same
dreary regard

the lobby at the gates
of Heaven is standing room only

passion feeds on
the hope of well-being

sad memories deceive
one's outlook

out-foxing hope
rearranging the rhythms of misery

the measure of my
soul
I cannot control

feasible limitations
suffocate
the extraordinary
bounds of the heart

don't let pain
destroy your dignity

Tearing It All Down Again

An independent will not of myself
but decidedly for myself
a will to recover

An ocean of sorrowful tears
I thought I would drown
the shore of hope almost out of sight
the reef of devastating oblivion
reflecting absolutely no light

Oh captain, oh captain
man the bow with a steady hand

Our depression is a wailing wind
the fickle saturated night air of the world
closes in on our weary ship

When, oh captain will we reach the farther shore
"the farther shore we are looking for" (Jack Kerouack)

Enlightenment
beyond life and death
the eternal self
non-self
the self of nirvana
the self of Heaven

The part of your consciousness
that will be the ideal self
God's self
let us pray

Sometimes You Have to Get a Little Drunk to Consciously Get a Little Sober

Among those who have come before
but have not considered the traces that lead their heart to action

I can't understand the makeup of my own ideas of fate
but things happen to me that I know will forever affect my fate
and I can't always feel this overwhelmed
with the prelude of glowing emulation
on the surfaces of impressionable minds
The countenance of true intentions
are far too often blinded by the
pride of sanctimony

Where must the moment rest within your mind to bring about the
unconditional dignity of someone
who is truly their fellow person's servant
to bask in the infinite dawns that globalize Heaven

Who at least begins their thought process in
non Autman (Non self)
these blessings that have been given bodies
can perceive the dreams of the
omnipresent
honoring God beyond the concepts of belief

and I can finally say in this moment of verse
that I'm finally ready to come back to the truest intentions
that magnify my soul

And all I can say to those who I parted from in a lack of closure is
that all is forgiven
and I love you as I always did even more in your absence
and all I can say to myself is that I should merely bide my time
in the hearts
of those who have been forgiven.

Eternal Notes

Freedom
fearlessness
limitable formlessness
nothing

May the beginning
beseech the end
and we all undertake
that which transcends
the wages of sin

Mere mortals
lollygagging

Fresh souls
crowding my heart

Where will I find
your emptiness?

Oh, angels
when must the infinite final persona
reveal its grandeur?

When must the
whole world
extend more than
it covets?

I have failed you, oh angel of death
caught in the agonies of Karma

Exiled in the subtle
reckoning of a hinted fate

Taking place
only to define the rest of peace

Peace is a Still Reflection of Love

approaching the final
journey
beset upon
the summation
of all your experience
the eternal notions
of yourself will prevail
over the physical representations
of how your world
acknowledges your presence

the grace of compassion
emerges
from states of suffering
setting one's spirit free

the expression
of every comprehended
thought

presents itself upon
the last breath

in this state of letting
go
in this state of becoming
whole

as one. . . as a family

we transcend all
differences in a state of
love

without

attachment
we completely
acknowledge one another
as one

the legacy
of effects that have
derived from the
conscious expression
of your life

will echo among our
most venerable
states of openness
for the sake of wisdom
tenderness
and acceptance

within the final experience
of this life we perceive and
see the nature of Heaven

within your own
love
which is unconditional
towards your family
there is the state
which will be your salvation
welcoming your very spirit
into Heaven

for I see no fear in
your eyes
even in states of pain

the humble strength
to which you so
subtly instill upon

us is more powerfully
relevant and apparent
than ever

without separation
we must all truly
see each other

without transgressive
limitations

we as your family
are of your very spirit and nature

will forever acknowledge your
intentions
rejoice for you are upon the
completion
of this your present state

yes . . . .
there will be no more pain
nor a single cause of expectation

this is your life

from which many have been
fortunate to share with you

thank you

Open to God

A tree could never account
for the number of leaves
it bears while in full bloom

Nor can a man who's heart
is properly open to God ever
be fully aware of the
perceptions he tallies
among selfless action

Reflections of unalterable
harmonies are kindled in
eyes of undeterminable illuminations
for beauty has a presence
beyond any meaning
and must rest forever

In every set of eyes
that are blessed enough
to open

Within myself I see
all of you dear strangers
and within us all I don't
see any questions

Hope is a Sunrise

don't let the devil shed
his shame upon your mentality

look grief in the eye
a willing recipient of suffering

do not encourage
the wages of sin

do not deny yourself
the possibility of recovery

within every
new experience
lies the hope
of eternity

Experience Varies from Manifestation
to Manifestation

from the things we lose our
trains of thought by

inside the displacement of time that
our heart beats between breaths

we know ample amounts of
our own presence

but to place ourselves in the
adoration of mere strangers

I anonymously and with
one iota of worldly regards
receive more blessings than
I alone should fathom

in every centimeter of
each movement
in the undetectable nature of
each second glance

the watchers personify
more mediums than
the impulses
that fluctuate
among the collective
unconscious awareness
of our species

Deep In It

The timing of opportunity is presented
by the opaque residues of deeds past in life
realizations of experiences surface in opiates of the spirit

A perception does not know
meaning internal absolute by
mere codes that prop the atrophied regards of the learned

A formidable mind blocks its subconscious degrees of intention
by the nature of associated thought
in the gray basics that are standards of judgement

The information channeled in objective introspection
can be woven together within the throws of the thoughtless
mind in a meditative arousal of the chakras
that of the eternal ruling class
the shepherds of our minds wait with their own delays
for this life will bask in the midpoint of the gate
where the earth knows itself by the mere cells
that are cast off by its patrons

The personification of the universal self
the innermost being is the understanding
of all beings what can be received is
the heaven known by the coexistence of the
earth bound

Heed the parallels that represent
such a world as this
in the eternity concealed within the breath
of a moment
All feelings occur by your own representations
of your inner and outer harmony and the
regard known privately within will accentuate
the subtle channels and ironies of a natural order

Building Foundations

I took a moment to consider just how much I
am not apt to perceive
in my regard for others and the regard they might reflect upon me.

When your heart capsizes because you just could not find
the right one.
The one who never thinks twice about convictions,
the one who's intentions
are uncharted and free from the confines of unquenchable desire;
desire which arches your will into the thresholds of
nitpicking greed;
desire which strangles up your heart, turning it into a seemingly
inexhaustible void that just wants, wants, wants, never relishing in
what it eternally will always have.

There are moments we ignore that will cater to the next life
when we learn to recognize these moments we can,
by our will make the provision
of acting based on wisdom
instead of the immediate gratifications of desire.

Layers over Grace and Solitude

The estranged likeness of a runt
strutting in fashionable death shrouds of myth and mercy.

Lay your head down old boy
that stoic ox can't pull your cart eternally.

Take some peace and quiet days
just to lie around and get your heart in line.

The world's damnable sadness
ain't going nowhere in this tomorrow morrow land dream.

You can choose your own flavor of deceit,
only a penny a pound
and the good little bastards of censorship will tally up their worth,
and rally around your feet,
and look up to you in the morning light
screaming God be praised, we've reached our common ground.

Although few will know of the hardship
experienced by the collective
with time droning on with its simulations of rebirth
ever beating themselves back like waterfalls in reverse, . . .
to that central pool in the streaming Akashic cosmic record
where all minds meet, and but a lone single heart still exists.

Seeing the Spaces In-between

The light that
consumes the Iris of the eyes
of fortune

discriminates far beyond
the proportions of
stable states of mind

among the present state
there are many
universally
                affected
revelations to account of
within the energies that
precede enlightenment

full awareness

of the feeling of
every arranged
molecule that
a spirit doth cling
to

screaming their
birthrights
        constantly
catalyzing their worst
        fears, the greatest
    desires wound in blind
            chambers of dis-acknowledged
    illuminations of the heart

the confines of inherent
mentalities are of the first

to be transcended in the
spirits release from the
            body
  one must distinguish
their nature
beyond the pull of predestination

subconscious plateaus of unconditional
awareness
ascend to conscious action

completely by the karma
inhabiting the spirit of the body it inhabits
and how it is presented in the mind
by the provocation
of the spirit

Escaping the Reactionary

Two opposing axes drawn from the same sphere
align to do battle, not knowing they are of the same sacred hoop

Must they be repeating this meaningless cycle for all eternity . . .
no, of course not.

The way has emerged and it will be taken up effortlessly
and merge
unaware into our consciousness, a holy afterthought.

Most will not quite be able to fully grasp it, but it will affect them in
harmonious and peaceful ways that they will welcome
and find great ease from
But few will ponder the great shift, the awakening of the masses into
a more responsible and considerate way of being

I feel that this is how true peace in integrated, with effortless ease,
let God take your hand,
the presence of God was in you all along

Babylon Falling Down

The great delusion of the masses
knives of misinformation, cannibalizing the
decency of the oblivious . . . disillusioned
souls bound thoughtlessly in the most detrimental
and venomous chambers of their own ego.

For all that is destroyed in the closing
of this dark age, it will be restored, to a much
more perfect standard, as the world peels
the scales from its collective third eye.
The people will no longer come back to what
has kept them bound.

People are finding new ways of living, the
paradigm has shifted, and the era of the
oppressive, patriarchal systems hell bent on
maintaining power through deception, subjugation,
division, covert manipulation, and exploitation . . .
that era is already dead, soon it will
be under the ground, and that which is of
the underworld will be returned to it.

Make Peace

Make peace with and give counsel to the nemesis of who is perceived as your enemy

The Meaning of Nothing

The meaning of nothing
the definition of everything
the thought of something in between is what counts

I remember more things than you wish you could forget

I never thought of life in terms of collecting memories
but I've accumulated more than I thought I would.
Don't let what's coming be a part of what's been left behind
Nothing virtuous causes pain . . . to anyone
Will this ever be understood by the world entirely?

Rapturing Daydream

Unestablished
doting fantasy

Coupled with your suffering
the seeds of supreme compassion

Saintly precepts
leave no traces

The beginning less remnants
of a soiled heart

Fortified to a continuous
notion of grace

When will you truly be able
to look at your own reflection?

He who finds himself
unscathed by desire
has the greatest appetite for contentment

Carry yourself in the true light of the world
and your shadow (ego)
will not confound your selfhood

I shall forever be a part of the light
just as all of us must be . . . .
hanging
        on
the end
       of
          time

Impressions upon Waking

A face you can't remember
but see clearly in your dreams

Expedient fate
my dance card is empty
a new bearing on consciousness
erodes itself out of a mountain
its peak is isolation
its valleys are the self-awareness
of a well contemplated mind

Turn your back to the sky
while embracing the warmth of the sun

The Hood of the Cobra

The hunting party arrives again . . . hungry.
The command of love from the fingertip of justice
Spirit horses take flight into the clouds, like crows on fire
heading toward the moon.

The mysteries of making the world whole
where the spirit moves the rest of reality follows.

Stingy, stale shadow hearts!
Brigandish misers saddle up with their foul atrocities.
False illumination is a keyhole you peak into with the wrong eye.
Cross the threshold and the doorway may seal forever.

The yielding tree sways in the strongest winds;
it bends effortlessly and with ease.
But the ridge dry brittle tree that will not move
with the winds of change,
that tree snaps in half with the strong winds of change.

Where did you plant your roots?

Aspiring Examples

Independently willful
the commitment of such an understanding
mind the gap, no gap

Extend the meaning of experience
deeper and richer
than the leaner foreground, that is obviousness

Respect the ways and means
of those who transcend karma
to inspire the masses

Immortal Karma

Complete yet unestablished
absent of a start
in the beginning-less sorrow
only you can convey
the limitations of your
own opinion of yourself

Nothing separates like hate.
The wholeness, comparable to divinity
is born of sorrow
and rooted in truth

Once established
it makes its impression
far beyond the grave

The Mysticism of the Moment

The moment you realize all you lost was
still there all along, it only changed form.

Form is a deceptive trickster
it leads us by the senses
not by the spirit.

The spirit is that of formlessness, boundlessness.
What is infinite takes all kinds of forms then continuously
passes them along, as the seasons pass, yet always reoccur.

Form is a wilting flower.
The world grounds us in form as the flower takes roots
the flower in its stillness gives off beauty
the perfume of the flower is a manifestation of the flower's being
existing in beauty.

When you awaken, all the mind is opened.
When you invoke compassion the spirit is cleansed.
You will live however many human lives as you need to,
to master this
(but like the video game Super Mario Brothers)
You can if you have the humility and wisdom,
find the warp zone, so to speak and skip to higher levels
LOL☺

One's own karma can be transcended, you have to reprogram your
ways of thinking at the root level of how your very thought patterns
are formed. You established these ways of ego-based judgement
based largely on lower, negative vibration levels.

Eliminate all that is based in fear, anger and ignorance; seek to tap into your higher self. The over soul consciousness that we are all a part of, each one of us a refracted spectrum of the soul of the creator.

Seek your intuition and discover your true powers of discernment, spiritual discernment, and intellectual discernment. The judgment you form in your mind will determine your fate. Be sure you do not mistake the true for false and the false for true. Most of you will, and have already, fallen into this trap in life, in all sorts of ways.

We must follow the path that preserves all life, and causes the least amount of suffering.

Don't Panic, Look Within

Rearrange your rationale
don't look for logic in gut reactions

When your desire attracts your greatest fear
you know you have not escaped the roots of what
binds you psychologically

Before patterns of behavior can be broken
you must first change the way you establish your trains of thoughts
intangible, impermanent self, . . . you can't repeat
what you have already lived
there is only now in the presence of now, don't find fault in the
thought of tomorrow

Seeing the patterns of the future by studying the past
lose the self . . . I need the nothingness
quiet, clear, without identity or thought

The butterfly stumbles from the cocoon
flying towards the sun

New Dimensions Merging

The wave collapses
awaken . . . release
potential
death takes the fire escape
myths blow the dust off legends

Dying lies
in sighing cries
lost in nothingness
your fear diverges
takes on new meanings
it traps your soul

Wretchedly deceptive old dealings headed out the door
The laws of reality and nature in shift,
and the direction is into a higher resonance.
Take it on higher now.
Lighten up and learn to be in love with the world
even though you may hate it.
You are it and it is you
and all the rest
God will have that too.

Awaken to What Now?

The dharma key has been thrown at your head
it landed with a thud

You may have known the mirror but the reflection alludes you
dismiss the weakness of the body, first heal the spirit,
then the body will follow
It is but a shell, a vessel; seek the wisdom of the soul in the
gentleness of the heart.

Reinforce these harmonies, the world needs magnanimous
compassion now, not tomorrow, now, and forever more.

Find it . . . seek until you find it, it's the only true reason for being.

Peace, love, light and harmony, it's very simple

Stop trying to make it difficult

Becoming Who You Must Eternally Be

The center becomes still as the vortex
surrounds all energies

Speaking clear and clean,
omens, so called dishing out contemplative turns
Facets of being revolve within the collective unconscious
a new standard for reality slowly falls into place
like the tumblers of a combination lock to the vault of the soul

You're lonely when you think of the past
the details add up to different circumstances in retrospect

The vestige of a dead totem,
its teeth crumble with the first bite of the divine
They are burning up like vampires at the first light of dawn

The shadow of a flame leaves only a smell
the directions of the winds are now rising to Heaven
The cosmic quarantine has dissolved. All divine love is slowly
finding its pathways, like all streams that merge into the sea. We the
salmon, swimming upstream, life after life, to reach the further
shore, "the further shore we are looking for," as Jack Kerouac put it.
Humanity will gradually, as we are ready, each of us in our own
time, find the perfect, still ripple-less pool to exist in, in love and
peace.

The Ego must be Distinguished from the Heart

Destined for disillusion
the souls of the mutually disenfranchised distribute themselves
sporadically and with the winds of discontent.

Don't dissuade your dignity,
don't let them compromise your soul.

Distinguish clearly your ego from your heart.
Don't display your insecurities on your sleeve.
Find your meaning in the stillness of your mind.
Find your wholeness in the stillness of your mind.

Don't allow the world to obliterate your state of mind.
Find your solace in your greatest state of happiness.

Don't discriminate!
Your essence transcends this space and time and will find itself
in the moment of recollection you will not allow yourself to
experience.

Distinguish the peace of the moment from the fears in your mind . . .
then dispel the root of the fear . . . you may recollect a sense of déjà
vu and that will remind you of moments you remembered your
nature, yet betrayed it.

You will be coming back to what you know and find it so inviting.

The Indigo Children will Take the Reins of Power

The gatekeepers of the great deception have lost the keys.

They are standing locked outside in the full light of truth.

But for all those within the "matrix" if you will, not only are the gates now open, but the very walls that held us all in place have all crumbled to the ground. We are being freed, things are going to change. It just hasn't sunken in yet, but the veil is being lifted.

What side will you be standing on when you become your own judge?

Come back to the source of your goodness.

A Total Becoming

A total becoming has many facets and new beginnings
Stifling the best of what once was
Tiny sufferings
Laymen mysteries of the discontented

Together they sail from one moment to the other
And find memories lost in recollection
Feasting on the violence of retribution

From the Top of the Head to the Bottom of the Soul

Eternity is like a flower that's constantly in front of our face the
whole time,
we just don't notice it.

Intention holds more power than definition
pain is temporary, love is eternal
life has its symmetries
the mirror mind
shattered shadow sides

Lack-luster measurements in the 3-D world
the geometry of the spirit
the side-saddled goddess has done hooked the stead to a chariot

Birth pains of a new era
what contrasts do you find within yourself
Can they meet somewhere in the middle?

If you are afraid to question yourself
you will fall for something simple.
I already had all the pain, the bottom doesn't mean shit to me,
I bought a fucking condo there.

I'll forever be pulling souls out of hell, until there's none left,
that notion warms my heart

I am just a man, but
I am a man

Summoning All that's Good

Summoning all that's good
Avalokitasvara, Jesus
Saint Michael
Don't be afraid of the confidence that the truth bears
Look out upon the world and know your virtue will reach the
highest heaven if your heart is true and ruled by love and
compassion. You will know the paradise, the nirvana, of a suffering-
less world one day. And when the great book is cracked open on the
final day, your name will shine out from within, not in gold but in
indigo like a prism of light that never stops refracting.
Practice the art
Do no talking
Leave no traces
You have only yourself
There is nothing else greater to master
Anyone on the true path knows the process is Infinite
And all paths diverge together eventually
And we'll all pass through it together as one when finality dawns
where all nothingness and beginnings meet

Gaps of Geography

Bridge the gaps of geography

Let Go of Anger

So many bad things begin with anger.
It is very easy to get caught by the currents of anger.
Though it is simple concepts I speak of, it can be one of
the most difficult things in life to master and take control of.

I highly suggest following this advice.
Do not allow yourself to act in anger in destructive ways.
It is a destructive energy, for all those who experience
anger. As Buddha said,
"Holding on to anger is like grasping a hot coal with the
intent of throwing it at someone else; you are the one
who gets burned."

Always follow the path that causes the least amount
of suffering in every single circumstance in life
that arises. Take daily actions if you're able, to
ease suffering, even if it's in a small way, everything
counts, so make it awesome.

Good Thoughts for the Future

Find the mirror of self, in every set
of bright eyes that are open.

Find the mysteries of the timeless
song of reality. Flowing waves of atoms
containing the black hole vortex of inverse emptiness
is somehow bonded to the nucleus, protons,
neutrons and electrons; spiritual energy holds
form together.

You can be both independent and part of the
higher good collective; some speak of it as the law of one.

We all live with habits and patterns of
behavior; it is how we construct our realities, around
the illusion of time.

When you practice the highest good, you will receive
the highest spiritual rewards. Every day practice
compassionate kindness.
If you practice compassionate kindness
to someone you hate, you are slaying
a powerful demon.

If you leave this life with a strong energy of hate in your heart, its
100% guaranteed to get worse for you in the afterlife. We have to
constantly clear our energies from the negativity of outside forces.
Fear, anger, aggression and all that spawns from it is an illusion and
a spiritual trap. Believe whatever you want, just don't fall into the
fear, anger and aggression trap. We are all one and all a part of God.
Don't destroy your spirit by trying to discover the nature of
victimhood. Don't delve into sob story notions of how your part of a

misunderstood special group that somehow places you above the common person.

Don't let knowledge cleave your head and form separatist ideas that create suffering. We were not put on this earth to find ways to separate ourselves from one another. We were not put on this earth to cause suffering. We are beings of love and light. We were manifested to add our puzzled-piece hearts to the infinite tapestry of creation. We were put her to harmonize opposing energies and create divine compassionate creator energy. When you discover the limitless joy of selfless service to those less fortunate than yourself the heart of divine creator compassion will begin to awaken in you. When it does, you must seek it and cultivate it every day, until one day you will do all this compulsively without even thinking, and when that day comes you will realize that you are truly deep off down the path of enlightenment.

A Retrospective Sunset

I have kept time with those who have to filter their
concepts of life within the trickling murmur of their own
predictable hearts.

And those who project their worries to lose their pain
will live their whole complacent lives in vain.

And all I see is never lost because it never stays the same

All that has passed me by I'll send on its way without bitter shame

For all things come back to us if we have no claims

I have been shallowed by those who misunderstand me
but I can control my dreams.
Most of my life was spent submerged in visions
that come and go within worlds.
I know form and how to change it.

I cast my mind out in search of a fear to
tremor the sanity of laughter
seven steps ahead is a will stronger than desire

The one thing that I lose sight of the most
the will of power
I have seen the pitfalls but ideas become
a version of reality sooner or later.

Seek Higher States of Consciousness

The lives we aspire
take root in the mind.

Allow the notion of yourself
obey the dignity of your heart.

Illuminating the understanding
of a communal, universal
consciousness

Established in the regard of whatever
the canopy of your
surroundings invites

Take into account all you may affect
among brittle personifications
the same way one would in
the presence of an auspicious
guide.

The synchronistic nature
of the vast spectrum of
fundamental human understanding
when one transcends their own
differences that separate them from
the understanding of a true experience
one is
ready to embrace
the heart of the Lord
the Bodhisattva
the majestic Christ
the prophet of Gabriel

the all-encompassing womb
of the great mother

An incarnate common man
universal in stature
consumed by experience

We Will Find Peace in the Future

Trillions of angry ghosts have joined the fray
the coalition is complete

I wouldn't want to be a dark heart in these times.

The chicken hawks have had their wings clipped.
The bald eagle has had its habitat destroyed.
Old Ben Franklin was right; the turkey would have been a much
better choice to reflect the nation's character.

The phoenix will rise from the ashes and birth a new world.
Fear won't change a thing at this point;
all it will do is just make things more painful for you.
Try to look for more solutions; take action.

Any hate you act upon will rebound upon you, so let it go,
you will only hurt yourself.

The Tree of Woe and Knowledge Merge

The sapling heart
emerges roots

Fragile and unaware
of the seeds that dropped
with the winds of previous generations

The burden of knowing
the how and why of existence
snaps back
in perplexing spiritual disorientation

And those that go through great pain,
must thrust upon themselves great change.
Then be born anew
the personality may shift

Old notions of false and harmful perceptions
let them fall away like the autumn leaves

With all that is discarded
not settled in the mind
stoking up the coals of determination

Make the choice.
Move forward,
even with the lonely that is you

You are the observer
I am the observer
of all these things we will take note!

The lullaby of lies
has not reached the soul
that's why one shines out

Follow the Buddha Nature

I awake, I imagine
I dream, I become

Fix your gaze between your brows
Sight your knowing in empty space
The way beyond the way is hard to articulate

Balancing the world on the tip of a needle
How much truth do you divulge to yourself?
What of your immeasurable self?
Each immutable spirit of humanity quells its on regard
and perspective
in the self-service of survival

But in actuality they are a part of a whole
that's unknown to them.
Endless lives can be wasted in ignorance
but it only takes one life of clarity
to purge the torment of the soul.

There are no divisions of consciousness
only the barriers rooted in karma and that which we make
for ourselves
one indelible degree of separation of understanding at a time

"See yourself in others, then who can you harm" (Buddha).

The one universal consciousness
seeks to be within your awareness
there is no division, no self,

Make Your Shadow a Marionette

Whiskey for breakfast at three in the afternoon
never felt so natural.

The sacramental inebriation,
a warm softness calls to me with its sweet light burn.
Jameson

Acrobatic time! . . . I'll smear the color of your meaning, . . .
internal becomes external, I know that jam

Pulling amusements from the spontaneity of an open old soul

When you think, deliberate and contemplate . . .
what is left to question?

Can you allow your perspective to willfully change and
overcome and adapt,
adopting a new way of being?

The path that leads to the least amount of suffering
is the long chess game

Can you avoid the reactionary
hop checkers calamities of the flexing ego brain

Our ancestor's traps tangle with karma
not of their own timeline
with ghosts suspended and mortals moving, fates get crossed
bleed together and often merge,
then emerge as one independent, external force

Emotion + thought = mental projection, give it some grooves,
a spiral and a direction

Find the whimsical state of consciousness
the one that takes you beyond yourself

In between a second thought, a clear mind

and the subconscious feedback of a staged reality . . .
let yourself slip through the cracks

Discover the vantage points that your mind will not naturally take
you to.

You See the Path as You Walk On It

Catching the sun
before it descends among our physical world
How much do you let pride harm you?

Do you render yourself
in the bitter reminders of previous pain?
Devious chains of naivety
Boy hearts of decades past
missing the mark
in the modern marketplace

There's room to stride in your own space
emptiness in your own time;
and a hymn, that distant memories
can't find ears to hear.

There's a purple rose on a gray beard
there's a faint laugh at an aimless map
there's a carousel of uncertainty in the lap of luxury

And mad children steal each other's futures
with blue moon regularity and
mechanical precision.

Distant hearts
turn back the tides
on a murder of crows.

And never cease the knowing
that always brings them back.

Mystic Imaginings

The world itself is derived within human
perception around conditioned responses

There are no rhythms nor order within
the cause and effect of our civilizations
that will provide for us
an outlook that will carry on into the afterlife

What a thing it must be
to completely transcend the physical world

We have amassed nearly endless extensions
of our own free will
and our complex and contrasted environments:
culturally, socially, religiously, and economically
all allow this world to have
a metaphysical chaos
for each energy within each one of
ourselves alone is divided in contradiction
and controlled far too often within the reactions
of emotional dis-acknowledgment in a conscious
display, mocking the very purpose of free will.
Learn to respond and never react

If we were conscious in the nature of our minds
in the full presence of the spirit, without the presence of our
five senses
we would be upon the most tangible revelation of the spirit
that of the realization
of the presence of the world in itself, as nothing more than
a projection of our own deepest inner wills of the soul

Many of us are not truly aware of the
absolute power that resides within the nature
of our will; one moment's decision
affirmed subconsciously through our inherent
conditioning can determine a spirit's path
for lifetimes to follow

For each moment of life carries with
it all the relevance of the hidden roots
of infinity . . . of eternal life
the full acceptance and realization of one's own ever
shifting makeup of energy without the thought patterns
and pre-assessed judgements and ideas
that falsely gives our ego a permanent sense of self
there is no self . . . death provides the business end of that
revelation to us all in the end

Once we move past the idea of this mortal coil
of birth and death of self
we manifest our absolute presence of spirit that found cause to
ascend to earth and to be born in the first place

The soul begins to take precedence and prevails over all
your intentions and actions

Your very being begins to personify in the cosmos
within this is the omnipresent nature and representation of
everything
which is the nature of Christ
the nature of Christ will save us

(People are too morbidly obsessed with the blood of Christ and how
it will save you.
I say focus on his nature not his suffering . . . besides he fully
understood the nature of suffering

which means he did not suffer . . . you can't lead people to salvation
through ideas of guilt.)

One begins to feel the presence of the whole world
as though one would
feel their own presence
one begins to strive to immerse their awareness in the
life force of every living thing

The patterns of nature reflect beyond
our earthly comprehension
the degrees that exist between us and the two mightiest extremes
that of Heaven and Hell
for both realms
are omniscient over all our precious frailties
and personified in all our earthly strengths

One cannot change what has never ceased to be

As all the streams upon the land of the earth
run off into the all-encompassing seas
that provide us life on earth
so must each our paths return to our creator

Chapter 2

Shades of Love and Some Despair

First Kiss Poem

Make me fall
make me bend
play me dead
roll me over
take me in

As I wash up on the
shores of your soul
once again

A Moment in Heaven

With floundering lips
of a magnanimous reprisal

I live in the wake of my
wandering fantasies within the unconditional language of the spirit
amassed to refine
the tactless symptoms
of control

And within a brief connection
of a gaze immortal
your spirit flutters
as my heart englobes
your very presence

An I rest in the
grace of such
harmonies

natural succumbing wills
that clear all processes of thought

With the exchange of an
unspoken kiss
that recoils
among the most
elusive intentions of
dreams

The Opening Bloom

The opening bloom
the thorns catch the skin
The rain mingles undistinguished from tears
The soil reminds the flesh of its final destiny

A solemn thought stirs the whimsical memories of youth;
it's how you remember it, not how it really was, like a sun bleached
scrapbook.
Musings of life casting shadows of mortality
The trunk of the willow tree knows not why its branches weep
A music box who's dancer will not spin
Displaying elegance in crude isolation
The name on the tip of the tongue dissolved in the bottom of my
heart
When I dream, I meet you there
When I awake, I see a mirror where reflections cannot be cast

Self-Reflection Takes the Day

Self-reflection takes the day
what madness you encounter will slide off your back

With the past standing on the footstools of dead love, trying to peek
into the windows of the heart

In the sickly sweet bated breath of dreams she holds me and cries
I'm sorry Ryan . . . I do love you.
I guess a continent of distance can't separate unconscious minds.

Though that which cannot die is unreachable to most it
cumbersomely streams from my heart with every breath I take.

Young hearts form so pure and then systematically become so jaded
from the banality of the nature of attraction and the ways of the
world.

We can all find it again, that pure, untarnished, unmolested heart
that formed within us during our awkward youth.

Drop the pretense and look within
look so deep that it scares the shit out of you
and dismantle those fears piece by piece, one by one
until your heart is once again without pain or misconception.

An Ode to Dorothy Parker

Stapled in dismay
putting every bit
of love to rest.

Saying goodbye to
the intentions I
thought best.

Enthralled, unfurled
a tender readiness
with no one to shelter my
loneliness.

Fate magnifies both virtue
and sin, a somber memory
balances a drunkard's grin.
I am due to fall in love again.

The Death of a Romantic

Repressed memories become past life déjà vu.

Pain spooks weakness, whipping excuses
to an incoherent stalemate.

No one
from no path
no-thing
drinking
lost eyes
peddled pilgrimages
leading back to the same starting point.

The shop is closed!

All I want is time and space
and no distractions.

Measures of activation
distributed precisely with dreams
and thoughtless interactions.

I have total freedom and when I share my heart everyone must think
I'm completely full of shit . . .
if they only knew.

The Primordial Communications

The longing of every human
  being to be soothed,
   caressed and erased
    from all that lies loathsome

The naivety of noble truths
burning as introspective
guides

Holding you in unbridled feelings
our eyes dance together inter-midst smiles
and endless facial expressions
We let it all go
just like the words
shhhh
    no more words
We'll let our energies do the talking
as the gap between your heart and mine
grows narrower with each embrace

Angels of Dover

Glutinous emotions
centralized to the pin drop ears
of premonition . . . the feathery vessel
to bring me a silence to settle in my grace

Your smile
cultivates the intuition of counter-acting personas

Revitalizing something I long since missed
one moment in your arms construes such bliss

In the spark of connection
nothing else matters when resolving
the pains in this reflection

In a moment of ageless perception
I see the rest of my life in such ample conception
brought to a halt is such disparity
on the brink of peace
brought by this soul ready to care of me

The mellow settling vibrations of a heart ready to mesh with mine
aura
calling out to me over the distance of memories

With your body asleep next to mine
of all the things I seek now I find

We Have to Say Goodbye,
but does it have to be Today?

A million ways to wish you well
so many thoughts in which I can't
find the reasoning
by which I have mended the idea
of where I left you

With but a single moment
to unknowingly exit forever
I begin to realize there is no
will to manifest this karma

At least not that leaves traces of those
still in bloom
and I must sway myself
in a dignity beyond form

Within the conditional fascination
of human nature
there exists a status of divine formulations

Tripping Memorials

What lowly, loathsome
temperament have I strapped on
in this most insane hour

Going mad beyond the solace of reason

In this same lucid memory
I can't stop rewriting the assumptions
of my enlightenment

Blinking my virtue
in such hellishly sadistic qualms
of all that ill behooves my fair dearie's grace

Just the right words
brought to my aid at the brink of my character's camouflage

The first impressions of love on the bypass of sensual delight

The Twelfth Circle of Hades

the indivisible
memories of my
unrequited beloved

years collect
themselves
with a hellish independence

the crime of not
loving one who
loves you

the brilliance of a single
hell enclosing in on itself
reaping the fruits of the broken-hearted

I cry as fates deny me
I wallow in the sorrow that renounces salvation of the mind

the tormented brood
new gateways of compassion

this is the only hope begot
of those who suffer in love

possess the restraint of angels . . .
not to suffer becoming a misery-less heaven

peace is final
rest assured

The Rationale of Weakness

Memories dis-acknowledged from the past
resurface leaving unresolved feelings
bare and unimaginable

A willingness to contend
lies dormant and unaware
the soul of the wit of longing

Must I forever be privy to my fears?
Inexplicably drawn to the end

Unfurl the damage
fashioned from the sorrows of wisdom

Lamented eternally
for a single notion of love itself
Immeasurable love
which shocks the senses

Is it somehow complacent
to love in vain?

An unrequited hell of a romance
all the disparity of hell
is inherent in what you can't have
but love ceaselessly

If you can forgive yourself
you can forgive anyone else
but only if you have true dignity

Living toward the moment . . .
even with the simplest of pleasures

One can survive in such ways

Self-Cleaning Chaos

her essence broods and curdles
from all the open wounds
she never knew how to mend

her eyes obstructed by scales
make the hope for herself unclear
her true beauty will never be found
in these same old depraved stomping grounds

to me it's the twisted appeal of bizarre
to her its home. . . . . .
but I like to leave my shoes there

Putting Yourself Out There

Establishing
the front line
of heartfelt sincerity

Re-establishing
a magnanimous
bravado servicing
the confidence of gods

Bring about the
sentimental regressions
of paradise
the inner murmuring
resonations of a wide-open
heart

I am the dream of
pure love here to
play its part

I bring you the brilliance
of un-compromised
feelings and intentions

With nothing left
to divide objectives in
contention

I am the rest of
your life in love
without convention

Om

A singular notion
of another's devotion
keeps me dreaming

I sigh inside
but kindle inspiration
with the endless fires of creation

Bringing me back from nothingness
without end

My new take on life shall begin

Longing

a thought of weightless esteem
a life most only breach
there are too many moments
between death and ecstasy
in this gasp of rebirth

with a glance she trembled
and I knew those eyes in the womb
of my eternal daydream

fantasy marries reality
in the rituals of my moods

a life that knows love
bears immortal ease in its passage

thought, as much as a heart lends, . . . lies
only the will of omnipresent clarity
shall negotiate the barren constraints of sorrow
and of extinct mentalities
she laughed sardonically
and knew in a moment what forever
could mean

our eyes meet open stirring incomprehensible daydreams
lifting our presence beyond earthly traps in the treachery of the
senses
and I knew in a moment what forever
beaming past all senses could mean

Bipolar

The greater part of one's earthbound self
ego-less in nature is impervious to sin

I myself like to bend the boundaries of both heaven and hell
Rejoicing in ecstasy, writhing in sadness . . . . . .

I compound my karma
gaining experience

Forsaken, forgiven
independent, dependent
an absolute monarchy of the soul

The thoughtless ethereal musings of discourse

Let me declare
my loves before I draw
my last breath
let me forget the meanings
that have gone dry
redistributing the heart

But my hands shall forever be on the wheel
the meaning of all final dharma is transcendentally available
to those who find themselves in the aptitudes of bliss
a passionless state of understanding

A truly selfless person inspires the great Creator

All or Nothing

foreshadowed in a moments
reckoning

misplaced by the cowering
lifetimes of those still in bloom

it's a long time coming
when you have a hard time
knowing just what you lost within yourself along the way

and you know
that I have a hard time
staying anywhere
for too long . . . . in these
God damn unstable states of mind

cause I'll give it all over
without provocation

and you know by now
it's so hard to tell just where
I belong

so thoughtfully bereaved
with the secondhand feelings of the present

O. T. T.

Confounded in circumstances
all is unwelcome in the eyes of the stranger.

The disability of heartaches
frozen in the heart of a stranger.

As the barmaids weep
wishing for lipstick lesbian tendencies

Tearing it open in the face of indifference

Does the drink belittle?
many say yes
yet,
what do they live for?
control
"control needs control like a junky needs junk" (William S.
Burrows)

Do we lose control to better understand where we stand?
Everything changes; we must to some extent change with it.

We will suffer much for what we can't change in our own hearts
but should.

I must remedy my homecomings with love.

Love's Serenade

Tender pale pebbled skin
the breath of ecstasy
the lip's impressions taming delight

All flushed radish red, the mind in one single frame
eyes closed, breath heavy

Stumbling onto one another
collapsing, merging into one wet fleeing aura

Independent, but temporarily undivided
the sultry sustenance, the jubilant escape
We should stay in bed all day.

Pacing Riverside

just another day
in this old ram shackled town

pushing hearts to corners just to see if they last out
with the same tired places and worn out bodies

slipping in discolored memories
far enough to nullify
the whole reason for existence

hip filled women
too promiscuous for their own good
these moments you forgot they re-wrote broken

in temperamental celebrations
I grow raw and dizzy
foaming at the mouth in some day-old fantasy

The Splendor of the City

The night reaches out in profound decadence
the effortless paths of excess
so jubilant and deeply satisfying

The beginning of an endless whim
the escape becomes so complete
the total justification of such naïve mirth and merriment
seems so worthy of praise in the moment

Nothing comes easy, hardships or blessings
to live alone in a narrow bed
devout with good intentions, sent in bad directions.
Before you can spread peace
you have to cultivate it yourself.

Thank God for this lifetime,
this space and time
the fruits of the Lord's blessings may take many forms

Though the streets burn with energies often caught in desperation
the women around the way make fearless eye contact.

There is an unknown certainty here; sometimes
the transitory visitor finds a home
in a world so temporary.

There is what was, what will be, and what remains
my spirit becomes transfigured with a million embraces
while never looking away.

Winding down the Night

Must we all be attracted to what we don't need?
I want to be drawn to a simpler plane
where desires are born in the wellspring of honesty
and fears are dissolved with mere explanations.

Never revoke an apology
close your eyes in the mirror and open your soul to reflection
place yourself in the world with no connection . . . to the agony of
that which can't find a home.
Don't tempt what's better left alone.

The luminescent pathways of night are wrought with excess and
failed connections.
Wallowing with a high head in an empty bed,
discordant separations breeding unreachable remedies.
How many formulas can be devised to apply to the fallacies of a
superficial world?

Reconstituting Broken Mirrors

Aimlessly
the empty daydream
takes hold in reality

Accelerated beyond
the most unstable points
of view

I hold my tongue
with impulses
that magnify thoughts
of you

Memory's jaded resolution
exacerbating circumstances
of my heart's confusion

I am the emptiness
one feels within the void

Happiness sewn backwards

Institutions crumbling
in a worldly pool
of sorrow and blood
the blood of an empty cause

An infant's birth cry
echoing its fate
an old man dies seeking grace

We all scare up a remedy
to go on
as the judgement of the world
comes too late

The Lost Causing Hefty Frustration

Take this moment and put it on a pedestal
Thoughts so dark they are light in retrospect
and dismal to disheveled recollections

This skewed state of understanding takes seed
in the moment you made yourself let go of
and I'll take this experience to be what you want it to be
and I'll memorize the lies you want to believe,
but I'm going to shun the grace and the peace that's in your mind

You'll never know the truth of the hearts you break
just find another fool to ride in your wake

And I'll make you fear all you have known
question the standard unto which you were born
This transgression
sealing your fate
The compassion you seek for yourself will come too late
How ya gonna spend your time
Deathly conspiracies making you lose your mind

It's a contract of shame
Are you going to sign your name?
Take the dignity out of your rationale
seek the sin as though it's not so sensational

Twist and bend the justification
Your reasoning is damnable
Your damage is irrefutable

Pray for what you do not understand
Cheat for what you take for granted
Ripping up your comfort like soiled carpet
I'm the enforcer of what you can't come to terms with
Reap the Karma of the herd you're in
Burn the field of the contentment you destroyed

Richly complacent to just say I don't give a fuck
You will wish you did
When you're all but dead
With no peace

A Time Slip into a Holy Union

A super-nova aura
coming through with cards
my moon sinks in your eyes

What perfect complements of grace could rest in your arms?

All my myths shatter in your presence.
What I knew ages ago, deep in the cerebral cortex was jostled lose.

Magnified with delight
the memory of an ancient or future civilization
when we were not so divorced from the divine.
The great foggy bridge to paradise.
My Lemurian bride.

Territorial Hauntings

There is nothing I can say
to make you awaken
there is nothing I can do to make you see the light

If you inherited an ounce of truth
your mind would surely be stifled
you would die alone in your sleep
with an aneurism in your head

I can't take the time to know you
You lie to yourself far too often
as you take the time for memories
and you shove um in my head

Saw you leave the bar last night
You stumbled on the corner
you looked so high I knew you
had to mistake your self-abuse for pleasure

There's not much I can say these days
and it's really kind of sad
Didn't have the heart to take you home
so you've got to put yourself to bed

I don't know what you're searching for
but I think you keep overlooking it

Don't act like you don't know me now
cause you know the scars are permanent

What you take me for is not this reality
the key to your heart's desire is betraying you

Transgression like a thunderbolt
echoing despair

What you think is so important
isn't really there

Unrequited

A great void of emptiness comes eating through with a simple song.
You will not leave my dreams no matter how much I sleep or how
soon I wake. These mental accessories are accompanied by an
albatross of memories too flawed to forget, that were too perfect at
the time for me to capitalize on.

I wish I didn't know what I can't get back. My heart set sail in your
eyes and my mind is a mausoleum where the relics of aspersions
take on the linen and liniment where drying flowers lay.
Even with this morose candor I have found new ways to live. Now I
see what you failed to see in me. When I knew you like the back of
my hand you never knew me at all. You only thought you knew me.
I never discovered my true identity until long after you broke me. I
have trembled within the little death of self-reflection, and dredged a
mystic hell gathering all the wisdom of
pain.

I am the last thought before you sleep
I am the thorn that makes you weep
The tearful embrace you will not seek
and I will no longer worship at your feet.
All we had is dead; who you knew is dead
only these dreams remain.

We were once one and the same.
I always know when you think about me.
I can feel it emanating from the center out.

Reminiscing of the Big Apple, and the Big Onion

I can remember a time
where wonders would spring forth
in the rejuvenating promise of a dream

I can still see myself there
New York City
harping on the faith of mankind
serenading strangers with my soul

Retracing the graces
of the brilliant
in the stomping grounds of legends
earning my namesake
delivering and receiving
inspiration at will

The indivisible delights
of a gracious metropolis

One More Floozy to be Forgotten

Expectations shattered
attractions scorned

The promise of a new beginning
stifled
by an unwillingness toward vulnerability

Will I ever have the luck of the committed?

Will I ever see myself in someone else's eyes again?

My longing is tone deaf

My keepsakes
have been abandoned

Memories resonate
with the hellish hauntings
of the unwanted, unloved
and unacknowledged needs of the soul

I ache for the company I cannot keep

I am a fool without a river
in a land barren of passion and meaning

Am I still at the bottom?

The Wretched Sorrow of Loving in Reverse

Reconstructing ruins
of vacant heartache
If you forget it somehow becomes
an even deeper part of you

So you maintain the grave of what
once was. Knowing you have known the joys of
pure paradise, what most will never come close to in this life.

And although you were there
in my mind we cannot leave
A part of me will always be there
Reconstructing you within my consciousness

A New Acquaintance

A new acquaintance
in oceanic eyes
as what's possible stretches out reaching for hope without suspect

New daydreams measure much
Humming melodies of the ancient symphony

Taken in, this open heart will not find fault

An Attempt to Put the Past Behind Me

Reinstated wellbeing
memorable acknowledgements

Forgivable pain
there must be no other kind

A heart thoughtlessly unbound

No more discordant heartache
oh great
Tathagata

Throngs of meager transcendence
find my way

When does one
transcend their own fate?

Magnify the faith
of the sweetest martyr
the brain child of salvation

Allen Ginsburg said it best
when he said
"The weight of the world is love."

We are what we love

The Escape Artist

Clearing old dead energies
stirring up leaves on a grave
Some depart, some stay but, all
get a glimpse at times
given the nature of one's previous karma

Devastating parasitic energy vampires,
sprinkle salt in your wounds,
oh, gentle memory lie to me one more time.

Desperate deserters build their own islands
Rudimentary outlooks fast track their half-lives

Songs buzz
Noise sings
Dreams harden like modeling glue

The geometry of heart break is stilted
It has no correct outlook.
Yet we return like the seasons
Just one more time, let me climb on this rollercoaster
One more time.

Scorched

They walk beside you
in your fantasy lives

She truly adores you
in the back of your mind

The young woman beside you
is the only one that guides you
through infernos and into cemeteries

To the apex of all that's
sane but illogical

You climb through time
and come to doors, enter
unknown realms of madness

Love scrapes a gash into your being
and you spill out all you thought was real
and the truth lies to your heart
and you drown in it

Chapter 3

Objections to the Absurdities
of a Misguided World

Red, White and Bloody

Endless executioners
exacting
their delicate revenge.

Feeble minded judges
stealing the limelight
falsely thought of as dignity.

School children imprisoned for profit alone
holy leaders with fascist crowns.

The tranquil numbing lies
rot with the most disgusting
pride and patriotism.

War is always unjust
and higher organisms
such as our species
should not propagate mass destruction.

Lay down your sins and beg for forgiveness
oh violent America.

By a Thread

Indignant frustration
Is this what you deserve
Got everything I need
But love is dead on the vine
My fate is stalling out
The loss of faith in the world
Doesn't come all at once
It comes a piece at a time
There is sacred life
But no one speaks of the life
That is less than worthless
Those that move in darkness
To angle their hatred at what they refuse to understand
They just can't let it go
And they're too cowardly to turn their pain inward
It's not so easy to block the outrage that comes from awareness

The Darkest Eyes and Awakening Minds

The season between illumination and disillusion
travesties contorting moral confusion.

Isolated . . . I see the chink in the armor.

Falsehoods, brainwashed hopes and disintegrating virtue

The nation has a sigh of relief within its own contentious heart
making marvels out of masochism, and legends out of lies.

You can't taste the drink, be it bitter or sweet,
for the nectar of self has no flavor
until the tears of the collective fall at your feet
and your soul opens to the knowing
of compassion that will not waiver.

Mass Mentalities have Treacherous Pitfalls

People don't become disillusioned by seeing the truth
people become dissatisfied by dis-acknowledging their inner truths
people dissolve themselves with toxic compromises
extinguishing their true mentalities
to assimilate the prevalent lies the world has taught us to obey.

When ego is recognized in the thought patterns, it is important to
make note of this and never follow it blindly into wicked
enterprises.

Your sorrow and your joy are not two separate emotions, but a
rainbow of the souls ungrounded nature, they are the same
until both is embraced openly and without suppression.

The ego will try almost involuntarily to deny sorrow
without pain and sorrow our compassion would be very shallow.
A person who denies their true self and true feelings is filtering their
percepts through a path that leads to wickedness.

Staring at the Oblivion of an Unknown Destiny

Staring at the oblivion of an unknown destiny
as though a self-moving path brought me here
This is where it's at
Oh the few that triumph and flower with their own self-fulfilling
prophesy
Deadly derailing thoughts
defeatism is its own disease

With the lost amongst the lost
and the dead that are in their grave
and that's the last place any of them want to be

Though we're contrary with this shiny new thing or that brilliant
new amusement . . . we cannot contend with what is going on
around us. As the cliché ostrich with its head in the ground, we live
our lives with our heads down, buried into digital portals
obsessively pouring over all the recorded information that's known
to man.

Whatever suits your fancy
but one day it will be too late to realize what's always been right
there in front of your face the whole goddamn time

Those Attracted to the Toxic

An angry ghost
dances a cumbersome
farewell, enchanted
by the dismal certainty
of human hearts
left wide open
left to die
weighing in
the perfect plane in your mind

It is always the same old story with me

the innermost circle is empty

no eyes to flower in

no breath drawing in on a heart's roots

to clasp the sweaty palm of destiny

I will not know a middle ground between peace and unrest

The socialized chambers of marvel

let me regurgitate you value systems

The noxious spirit-tarnishing remedies
for the collective unconscious
with enough brutal vanity to poison

So many pure intentions
disabled by the courtesies of the ego

The Lost and the Angry

More fodder for your moral quandary
the dotards delight, the profane becomes sacred
as minds are lost into delusion and hate.
The spoiler of souls placates the ego to bind the psyche
a primrose path straight to the gates of hell.

Did you make a conscious decision to shed your common decency
to further your own self-interest?
You better hope that's not the case for your sake.
Though some can transcend karma and much is spoken of this and it
is emphasized as much as humans transcend bad karma, they also
descend into profane detrimental negative karma.

Don't let anger, fear and ignorance allow your ego to tarnish and
condemn your soul.

A Dark Chapter of History

It returns
like an admonished friend you now find disdainful
like an infection you thought cured that regains its festering rot
it offers you simple logic, logic and a piss poor lack of will and
energy

I unconsciously perhaps, have largely isolated myself from the
world. Like a lone man sailing the open sea

Torn from your dreamer's soul were the days of wonder and divine
passion and those feelings that could never make jaded the
perfection of love

Today's world has forsaken the dignity of humanity, and America is
on the chopping block of karma.
People are sacrificing their decency on the altar of fear, anger,
ignorance and hatred
Therefore you have lit the fire that will one day consume you in Hell

You misguided assholes elected a narcissistic, megalomaniac,
sociopath who is also a sexual predator. An evil, delusional lunatic,
that's what Trump is.

And now everything is going to get so much worse. God is
punishing us. I have very little hope for the future
and maybe as a country, this is what we deserve. We have been
complicit or supportive while over half of our tax dollars go straight
to killing people in the Middle East for too long.

The great empire has tarnished our spirits.
We are deceived then taken advantage of.
Change cannot come fast enough.

On the Grind

How vehemently we ponder our death
how flippantly we live our lives
dredging up the routine
Are you late for this moment?
Are you too early for yesterday's dreams?

Dealing for the dollars
peddling away the hours of the day
with the system slinging its standards,
straddling both the predictable and the random.
What sense does it make?
Are the lies you will not acknowledge endangering your soul?
Few in Hell thought they would end up there.

The Spiritual Evolution is Not Yet Over

Intangible lucid daydreams
meddled with green smoke
with blood in my mouth and whiskey on my breath

I can taste a whole new thing taking over me

The truth of justice would murder your dreams and ideals
how frail and damnable are the things men hold sacred

The abominations of pride carry with it much suffering
suffering upended by suffering

A butterfly effect on the karma of the soul

Will you stand on the side of death
or on the side that preserves life?
Preserving life is a more sacred thing than pride or principle
or any sycophantic notion of vengeance

Or is the sheer genius of forsaking yourself
just too alluring?

We come into this life screaming and in frightful agony
then we all dream of leaving this life
with not a whimper but a sigh of relief

Oh how we long for a more perfect life
in death

Or a more dignified means of believing in faith
the travesties of divisions of hate
separatism . . . .
The face of God still goes unseen by human beings

The name of God and the meaning of that name
still remaining un-inscribed in the collective psyche of our species

Must we awaken with every generation
marred in our course to the sins of our forefathers?

The Past is Not One

The rubber toughness of idealism
how many chances do you get to be a sucker
the analog of treachery
the bad karma of misanthropic destiny

Shred my consciousness
into a state I cannot recognize
the cost of unhappiness is paid for with a universal currency
the peace of compassion taunts me
with the unbearable natures of attraction

As the aspects of your character fall away
a new personality emerges
who we are, who we were, and who we will become
can will alone steer my course

The ways of the world have lost all fairness at times it seems
feeling the need to meditate well into the void
the darkness of damnation, the absence of elation
staring at nothingness like a child with his nose in the corner

I take my life lessons for more than they are

That Fateful Day

Exercise your livelihood
with a clear head

Extend your selfhood beyond
your own internal nature

A becoming must never
cease to become

It's our hope to cheat death

Death is the last transformation of this stage

Death ushers us away
like a sleeping family in a bomb raid

Death the messenger of fate
Death existing within the principles of irony

Consent your gray beliefs
to the acceptance of an impermanent world

The confined, loathsome agonies of life's conditions
are extinguished and reborn moment to moment

Standing Strength Picks up the Pen

Down to the base of the wick;
I got the braves on charge exponentially

The spirit of hawk
talons seize like razors
in the minds of the wicked
and so it is done.

The judgement!?
The scales of God's judgement soon to activate
In the hearts of the collective, while we live and breathe
You will become your own judge.

I hope you choose wisely

Gossip Girls

Gossip girls
Your cunt doesn't glisten so well in this light
The competition will not be annihilated
It will be white-washed into nonexistence

The truth be told in dreams they mold
Like mausoleums excavated in proletariat delusion

Symptoms of the disavowed
Hollow homeless
Fractured spirits

Disciplined as field mice
Clinging to the falsehood of past realities
The lost remain that way until they find themselves

Three Into One

The shadows of pain
with the awakening of the subtle body

When you don't have to look for what's dead inside,
because it goes right ahead and presents itself through society.

Not too far, it ain't so deep
the shame of ego.

Your frustration and ignorance
it draws you up tight, as a firing pin . . . cocked.

Lies unravel
hate fizzles out
An ouroboros destiny
Oh, dear God, the disdain,
the irony . . . in all this endless mental projection.

Perceptions are going to shatter;
you backed the wrong horse.

The divisions you create are not a part
of true reality.
Your embroiled mechanisms of logic
are feeding you only hate.
And now the house of cards will fall.

The quicksand ideologies being peddled
will swallow up even the slyest of souls.
The mass marketed hubris of the emotionally mismanaged
too woefully terrified of introspection to object.

The mirage of better days drags the carrot on the stick
out over the cliff, Fox news provides the fog.

It's time to separate the wheat for the chaff
and the swine can have their pearls,
we will take the oysters.

We are the only ones who can reach them anyway.

The Great Awakening of the Masses

The bright warm measures of dissidence
the perennial patriarchal oppressors scramble to make
nonsense of common sense decency.

They knew all along that they
were burning a candle at both ends.

What they didn't count on was
that the focused rays of the light of God
were going to melt their candle from the center out as well.
Expect eminent pools of wax.

That day is done dog
fuck your evil candles.
Clean up your mess
and get the fuck out.
You callous ego-brained assholes
We don't want your devil philosophies
anymore, to paraphrase Bob Marley.

A constitutional crisis,
a crisis of faith.
We have let the shit rise to the top
but now it's going to run downhill
and back to the cesspool from which it came.

We, as societies, have suffered the hypocritical indignity
and disgrace of your evil, deceitful ways
for far too long.

The paradigm has shifted
your wickedness is now in retrograde

your old ways are null and void
and they will be abandoned.

The Fall of the Roman Empire,
(The Essence of the MAGA Cult)

Alone the man stands
wrapped and bound within anger and fear
with no sanctity whatsoever.

No belief apparent in his heart
in this the most violent culture in the world
his will carries over with
the stench of Hell in the prevailing winds
of such a vacant and transgressive mass-mentality
he never yields to any
for he has never reveled in the omnipresent qualities of human virtue
in his unwillingness to succumb to empathy,
benevolence and remorse
he harms far too many

His head filled with moxie and spite
he cackles and is amused by the suffering he causes
this to him is the sweetest thing in the world

Indeed he has lit the fire
that on his final day will consume his spirit
he has no tangible identity in his momentary wicked delights
he cannot live with his pain so all he knows to do is cause it
he never questions himself
he sees weakness as strength
and strength as weakness
he loves only himself and
abuses all that come to love him
like all demonic forces of this plane

he is a deceitful coward, illusive
and unaware of anything but himself

As history shows, the greed of capitalism
secretly turns the weak minded
populous into elitist pigs

What an extraordinary thing it is to be born a human being
what a tragic thing it is to squander your life with notions of
outrageously extravagant self-gain
swept along by the currents of Hell
he puts his wrath in place where his forgiveness should be
over and over again

Motivated completely by lust
he sees disgrace as honor and honor as disgrace

People of virtue weep for such men
lost among their evil nature

And as our damned
country becomes more and more fascist with its
greed
it breeds so many impressionable desperate
young men
into psychopaths
but since most of our politicians are sociopaths
with no conscience whatsoever
I suppose it's all too relevant

S. S. D. D.

A clamoring disassociated
unimaginable state of affairs

Where is the endless new beginning I long for?

The curiosity of my heart was born
with all the questions reasons will allow

Imagining myself
I always see more than circumstances
will allow.

Just, Why?

Does the collective perception determine the future of
excepted reality?
Did we drive off into some dark parallel universe?

This just in:
In attempt to outdo the race to full on deranged, the GOP has
announced they will be running Alex Jones in 2020. The pentagon
says it's imperative that we do not develop a derangement gap in
relation to other dictatorships like North Korea. This, as president
Trump and Kim Jong Un continue their public media feud over who
will be the first to usher in the apocalypse. The department of
defense chairman stated, "American exceptionalism will not be out
crazied."

We know them by their deeds,
but far too many only believe their lies.
When we lose our humanity, democracy dies.

March On

Immeasurable
destructive sadness

The melancholy shackles
of those in mourning

Mourning the dizziness of war

The predisposition of those who take a side

A violent death cannot rest

Not in patriotism, nor martyrdom

Nor those who
despicably say "For Freedom"

Duty and honor
are absent without compassion

We all bleed the same color

But compassion,
compassion will save us
sure as a bullet

We must all beg for forgiveness
in the name of all who have fallen

A Whirlwind of the Times

The four horsemen ride on by,
their grandeur and reverent cataclysmic
oblivions demand more respect.

The gods don't accept bullshit.
We know the truth and future generations
will be born just understanding it intuitively.
The information is out there, justice is
a part of karma.

The new paradigm is no longer going to support the systems that
promote suffering for profit or encourage 1% of billionaires and
near billionaires to own and control half the world and its resources.
They are playing god and it goes to sociopathic insane lengths.

Money over everything, including compassion and human decency,
this is the unspoken gold standard of modern American corporate
culture. I have dubbed it cutthroat capitalism. America has officially
taken its level of capitalism to disgusting, terrible lengths. It is no
longer a democracy; it's a fascist corporate oligarchy.

Snake Charmers and Hodgie Hunters

Drinking in Clarksville, downtown
where the jarheads examine the college boys
as though they were exotic colorful song birds that
have never been seen by human eyes.

They all congregate and huddle like a herd of silverbacks,
and sometimes one will get far too close to another one
and they expel unnatural human-like sounds at great volume
making everyone jump in their seats for a moment.

As they inhale their golden and amber bubbly brews
they search for manhood and swap stories of state sanctioned
violence.
Ah, the glory that is Rome!
Conquests may never cease
an erection looking for a hole.

And for the night, death takes its R & R
and the blood spattered faces that can no longer scream
become a little more bleary in the distorted dreams
that haunt the empty shells that were once men.
As the night wanes into morning
the taxis round them up, some of them carrying others
who have long since puked and turned pale in stumble-bum
decadence.

And those of us who have retained our individuality
just shake our heads as we walk away having downed the last call,
thankful that we did not become the enemy on that night.

Leading a Horse to Water

There was a time
when nothing was separate
the root of all our minds is still grounded there
in the dormant parts of our DNA

Order was created because chaos is feared
by the linear mind.
Piece by piece, slowly, often times by attrition,
Society chips away at the defamation of our souls

Inconsistent geriatrics
with cannon fodder, cobweb brains
they don't want to give up the river of blood and suffering
that they extract from those that they see as peasants
Mere food for the corporations

Bottomless suffering, bought and paid for
MAGA equals lock up the foreigners
as long as they are brown people who are poor

They kidnap children at the border, this is the order's new disgusting
standard
and it should not be upheld, we should all speak out against it.
It's judgement day and the choice is yours
this karma we are in now is like a surgeon's scalpel,
and the cancerous tumor will be removed.
Winston Churchill said it most succinctly when he said, "America
will always do the right thing, after they have exhausted every other
option."

2020 The Year of Mass Death
and Mass Delusion in America

Automated grave diggers, denial of reality keeping you at risk
laying out the myths of ideals rooted in deception,
for their internment into the oblivion of lost souls

"Let them eat cake"
The sweet taste becomes muted by a bitter poison
there's no almonds in the mix, and no fillers for the heart
pumping a cyanide sayonara to the compassion
morals tried to impart upon you

I incite riots of the heart
for the sake of the soul of humanity
Expel the separatism, exile the ignorance,
before it leaves you stranded in a world of evil illusions completely.

The Sage Walks Away

The crown is open
in the wet dingy morning light.

Faint in dark space
the verse and the inverse tug away.

The memory of a feeling
a smile
a sudden attack of iris
the exhale has been taken out of me
I was not aware.

Speeding into a stale synthetic oblivion
this veil was a mere curtain on a stage.

The dreams we live and the life we dream;
does the contrast become lost upon awakening?

Terror chases freedom round and round in a circle
until we all fall over dizzy.

Without wisdom there can be no prevailing triumph
only bondage.

We were not put here to separate ourselves from one another,
lost without direction.
I sit silently under the biggest tree in the forest
and forget there was once a path.

Take the Slack Out of Your Jaw

The rope-a-dope winds
derange a pleasant distraction
for the tarnation of the masses.

Clawing, shifting, slipping
cutting cords, disavowing division
their scales were contaminated by eradiated
angry ghosts

The channel has been opened,
the stone has been removed.

Confined dystopian myths
you forgot about greed, ya dummies
now it is all you are.
Endless desire leads to Hell
every goddamn time,
as sure as a bullet.

Megalomaniac Nation

Absolute power
will devour
the sleekest of souls

Moments devise themselves
independently
nothingness enclosing
in on itself

The pity a bad mother
shows her children

God remembers each
of our names
in the luminous fetters
of an individual soul

Fashioning reasons
to be
all is lost and
found to be controlled

Still my senses will not
relieve the sensation
of the truest of loves
that ever begot
creation

To find your heart
without the world's
relation

A thing a poet gives
much contemplation

My salvation will come
with nothing less than
losing myself in the
throes of revelation

Myths of Mars

Lists are read aloud
wheat from the chaff
guillotining fate
summer salt whirlwinds

Wrath rearranges symmetries
. . . the snake behind the snake

Who struck where?
Dispensation's mask hides eternal

Your core is what you made
the date was much too late
exhausted ones collapse as their souls fly high
the dreams unwind the serpent's lies
the death knell stroke comes from all sides

The Ego Lies?

Embracing the slithered wreck
of such cognition
surpassing actuality

Clamoring to a sense of immaculate perception
drowning in the lifestyles of your neighbors
conception
brought on yet restrained in recollection

Isolated from contemplation
lies conviction within your own soul

And so you stride far beyond character
the ego extreme diverged and lifted to alter
in the exuberance of optimism

so uncontrolled in this state I've induced
to remedy my moods

Only Stupid People Get Bored

eclectic, uneducated
blind idealists
collecting their simpleton dreams

the dreams they are force-fed from childhood
the carbon copy remnants
of the damned and disillusioned
seep back into the
quickening existence
of vengeance alone

we will earn our weight
in blood and bullets

"if you hurt or grieve another, you have not learned detachment"-
Siddarta Buddha

don't let fear limit your understanding of the truth

Intermission

Desensitized
dissatisfied
cool jeweled new illusion
consciousness expansion
wallowing in monotony
hit a wall of boredom
bask in dreams
untold sentimental celebrations

Life is but a colorful
simulation of a series of emotions
written through a story called time
now let's pause and laugh at the ones we missed

Bright empty days
nights filled with lavish extravagant
ways

Are your dreams too convenient to grasp?
You can't tell one day from the next
your life has elapsed.

Do you hear clocks ticking when there are none around
if time is but an illusion
perhaps it's the places we're in
the old headstrong individuals
the ones you call your friends

Someone goes away
you await
for new planes to build your heart upon

I await the true meaningful life
for now I'm stuck somewhere in between
and completely sober.

One of God's Prototypes

The beginning of nothing
thoughtless patterns of logic
emerge improperly

I can't contend
with the sense of this experience

To revel in absolute beauty
and to be personified by divinity
one must be absent of the impact of the hellish rejections

I can't remember the namesake of my title

I can't defend the contempt of my heart

Only God knows my true identity

Chapter 4

The Prose

A Simple Philosophy for a New Age of Peace

War is like a cancer. It should be contained locally and should never over extend localized reach. The invading army is always the bad guy; if every country lived by that rule, that the only way a country should engage in a war is if some one's crossing your border and entering your back yard, there would be no goddamn war. But if one country invades its neighbors the countries that come to its defense should only be the ones surrounding it. Killing is killing, it all results in tragedy and pain for all those involved. Don't allow yourself to kill for a cause or because you are ordered to. If everyone who was in our armed forces banded together and said we won't fight we will not fight in your wars abroad only if there's an invasion of America, our country, we would be through with war for now. As it is, we are creating tons of bad karma by what we're doing now. One day we, collectively as a country, will reap what we sow. And it's not going to be pretty.

Sometimes it's Unbearable
(written around 2010, statistics updated 2023)

Our societies are beset from every angle with towering monuments of evil; and they have always been there. From the first time each of us ever opened our eyes there it's been, looming in the foreground. We have become so used to it being there that we don't even see it any more.

Human beings seem to have a deep seeded unconscious or subconscious impulsive need to shave off the edges and frays of the population with sacrifice, human sacrifice and suffering, human suffering. We harvest this suffering; we harvest this sacrifice with labels of ideology, with justifications of our belief systems. We rally round notions of God, justice, revenge and patriotism as they feed us our daily helpings of government sponsored fear, and we pay the tithing of our collective dark hearts and we destroy. We destroy lives with discriminant precision; we destroy the poor and the disadvantaged with our court system. We have become as Hunter S. Thompson put it "a nation of jailers." We imprison more people than any other country in the world. Over 1.2 million people are incarcerated in the U.S. (Carson, E. A., *Prisoners in 2021-Statistical Tables,* Bureau of Justice Statistics, 2022, bjs.ojp.gov.). The U.S. makes up less than 5% of the world's population but we have roughly 20% of the world's prisoners. One out of 5 prisoners in the world is incarcerated in the U.S. (Wagner, P. and Bertram, W., Prison Policy Initiative, 2020, https://www.prisonpolicy.org/blog/2020/01/16/percent-incarcerated). The prison population has doubled since 1985 because of our nation's draconian destructive drug laws. This must change; we must make them change the system and do away with so many of these concrete slave ships that are our prisons.

Then there are all the wars we have started. We kill far more of them than they do of us. Approximately 300,000 civilians have been killed in Iraq over these last two bloody decades (*Cost of War*, Watson Institute of International & Public Affairs, Brown

University, https://watson.brown.edu/costsofwar/costs/human/civilians/iraqi). How would it make you feel if you walked outside right now and saw tens of thousands of dead children lying all over the ground surrounding you? Would you feel like a good Christian, knowing your tax dollars paid for the war that caused their deaths? Don't kid yourself folks, the war was fought so the corporations could profit from it and so they could get an economic foothold in the region where all the majority of the world's natural resources are located. Every other reason they give us is pure lies and propaganda. They never let a great tragedy go to waste. They use that same old tired Hegelian dialect formula on every other generation and get away with it. Create a problem, get a big reaction out of the public, and stoke the fires of outrage with inflammatory propaganda, then present them with the solution which is their already prewritten agenda, which they could not have gotten away with doing without the horrible tragedy that put fear and hatred into our hearts. Wake the fuck up people. The people who start and maintain modern wars are agents of the worst kind if omnipotent evil power because they are beyond reproach and are not held to account for the death and devastation that their orders bring down in this life. The very worst part of hell will be reserved for the architects of these atrocities. It's time to take the power back and free the collective human spirit from the bonds of fear and anger, for they lead to the dark side. Didn't you geeks learn anything from Yoda. I know this geek did. And for those of you who say oh all that's absurd you're full of it, or if you are offended or can't see the truth in my words guess what.

You're a sheep . . . and the sheep dog is speaking to you urging you to not get startled and blindly run off the cliff with the rest of the flock.

Collecting on Nefarious Contracts

The old evil forces in this world are being exposed in the full light of God. They can no longer hide their great grids of separation and deception that have kept us all in bondage for thousands of years.

The Christ consciousness is awakening within us all. It cannot be stopped by machinations of science or by propaganda. It is a vibrational energy level. It's built into your DNA and your brain. The world of mammon and physical form has absolutely no dominion over these changes. It's going to be a future of enlightened spirituality. We will live personified within this three- dimensional world in the full God energy of our hearts and souls. Our compassion and kindness of heart will rule our minds consistently, eternally. This is the key to becoming the individuals we must eternally be in Heaven. This is the key to Heaven on Earth, and we were all born with it.

Amen

Notes on Navigation

Consider the benefits of detachment. Emotional involvement should be guarded but not the understanding of human nature. That is not to say one should continuously remain a casual observer. Bide your time . . . and know your moment in time and the full nature of the context of it all and then if so inclined, act accordingly.

Know when to speak and when to listen, when to teach and when to learn. And most important of all, learn when to shut the fuck up in order to stay out of trouble. Not all knowledge is for everyone to know and some opinions are better kept to yourself. It is wise to avoid angry conflict. Always consider your audience and how best to reach them. Few people truly have free thought, most follow one learned perspective and the logic that it entails, and they don't like their beliefs or the rationale that goes along with those beliefs to be challenged. It's no wonder our species is still waiting on the great mass spiritual awakening to balance out our many ages of reason. Some can eternally awake in this life but for a great many it cannot happen in this lifetime. Think for yourself and question everything, yourself most of all.

Try to be Optimistic

Take responsibility for everything my friends, everything in your world, whether or not you affect it directly, indirectly or not at all, truth will come to light eventually, and bad karma stands on the wrong side of truth.

Even if your voice is heard by only one person,
a jug fills drop by drop and so the wise man becomes full of virtue, but the fool becomes full of folly so says the great Siddhartha Buddha.
Be the one who turns deals into peace and anger into remorse.
Try not to dismiss those who are opposed to you for as much as they are opposed they are more similar than your reason will allow.
In life those who are emboldened with passion often make their mark but miss the mark of finding peace within themselves.

I am guilty of this.
A man who questions himself refines his qualities and roots out his misgivings.
Break free of cause and effect action and reaction.
This is known as mastering one's reality and breaking free.
Find your moral compass by looking deep within, not by learning from the world.
Your truth is yours not someone else's.
To thine own self be true as old Shakespeare says.

Thoughts about God

If God is infinite and eternal, wouldn't it stand to reason that God therefor would have infinite manifestations? What is of love, light, compassion, forgiveness, kindness, truth? I believe this is what's of the highest good. Just remember awakening is painful at times, take it easy with yourself even when others act like assholes. At the end of the day we are all one anyway. Just fragments of God's consciousness . . . so why quarrel?

Who Are the Real Bad Guys?

In America almost everyone has been brainwashed into believing that when you go overseas and fight in another man's war, or when you invade another man's country, that you are serving your country.

In fact you are actually fighting the men who are defending their country. You are not defending your country. You may be fighting alongside another group within a country against an opposing group. Or you may just be fighting to expand your country's empire and benefit the war profiteers.

The New Way Emerges

They have driven our institutions into a ditch.

The powers that be have allowed their avarice filled greed and lust for power to destroy so much.

It's up to us citizens now to vote them out of office. Until we take the money out of politics the grifters and those who wish to abuse power and exploit the earth and its people will always rise to the top, like a turd that won't flush. If we continue on in the manner we have been, if we obey the status quo and go along to get along, our society will perish.

We will change; we will cut away the cancer of corruption. We will bring in a new age of compassion. Their evil works can no longer be hidden in this new emerging age. Too much information has already been disseminated. You can't put the toothpaste back in the tube as they say. It's game over for these parasitic pieces of shit.

The great upheaval will be one of the mind. Perceptions will shatter on mass like contrary glass houses. What will shatter them will be the voice of God, revealing the truth and unraveling the great deceptions of society that took over a hundred years to root in the zeitgeist of our culture, as the great saint George would say, "It's all bullshit folks and its bad for you."

Manifest your own new realities. Like they said in Dune, "fear is the mind killer," Don't live in fear, find joy and live in happiness. It all starts with your own thoughts. "Your worst enemy cannot harm you as much as your own thoughts left unguarded. All that we are begins with our thoughts. With our thoughts we shape the world. Speak or act with an impure mind and trouble will follow you as the wheel that follows the ox that draws the cart." – Buddha

Do the work that brings you joy and fulfillment. We all have our own unique paths, we must all find them on our own to find fulfillment to a large degree. If you seek eternal fulfillment you should seek that of the soul or spirit. The path of self-mastery has many gateways that change one's character. With self-mastery comes self-awareness. Then comes awareness of the world and the true nature of reality and how it is manipulated and controlled by those in power and by those with the most money. There is an order to it all and the model it is based on is that of slavery. Do you think the cows know when they are in the slaughter house? You think they know what's coming?

Now is the time for the awakened to step up and speak out and "be the change you want to see in the world" as Gandhi said. It's our time, it's ours for the taking, it's needed and it will be done.

Find All the Many Fibers of Your Being

Find all the many fibers of your being that are made up of goodness, kindness and all that humanity should eternally be, and examine them carefully, study and meditate on that compassion.

And then when you're standing on the cliff of life afraid to take that next step, when you're surrounded by darkness, know that the light that will reveal the ground beneath your feet as you must take that next step will come from within you and exude out of you prominently, the eternal truth that's ingrained in each of our very DNA. We are the light and we must magnify it until the darkness is banished from even the faces of the deep. When you find a true connection with every living thing you will know the heart of God. Try not to cause suffering no matter what the reason. And do not do evil for the sake of good.

Things are Changing Faster

Things are changing faster than society's standards are able to keep up, the paradigm has shifted. A new age is dawning and mankind is shedding the scales from their eyes and finally starting to see the truth about the world. The genie is out of the bottle, too much truth has been disseminated, the lies that keep us oppressed will not hold much longer. That's why the NSA is monitoring all the information everyone looks at over the internet (which is an oracle). They want to know who knows their dirty secrets. The day will come soon where the age of mass deception will expire. For all that is hidden will be revealed; evil has an expiration date but the divinity of goodness and truth is eternal and unalterable. There will come a day probably around 50 to 70 years from now (2015) when our society will no longer accept, follow, or stand for the evil that the powers-that-be force upon us. The Hegelian dialect will become ineffective; the divide and conquer methods will be rendered useless. If they can make you believe separatist notions they can make you hate identifiable groups of people. If they can make you hate they will lead you by your hate, straight into Hell. What part of "all are welcome at my Father's table" did you not understand you dumb ass. It matters what's in your heart not what group you were born into. For the first time in a long time the new generations, the millennials and post millennials, are turning away from organized religion to seek God. I think that's the way it should be. That's the path I took long ago. Look within yourself to find God not to the church. The church creates a barrier between you and God by getting you hung up on separatist bullshit like hating and judging different groups of people. Nothing virtuous and of God causes pain to anyone. Don't persecute people in the name of God, you're doing the devil's work. With awakening comes disillusion, then outrage, then you have to repent and turn away from what you didn't know was wrong. Most people's ego won't let them admit to themselves

169

that they have been following the wrong path, therefor they do not awaken. How many lifetimes will you be lead into bondage before you take responsibility for your own thoughts and lead yourself to salvation.

Made in the USA
Middletown, DE
03 October 2023

40113719R00102